EMERGENCY ROOM

Emergency Room

© 2021 Alan Britt

All rights reserved. No part of this book may be reproduced or transmitted in any form or by any means, electronic or mechanical, without written permission from the author, except for the inclusion of brief quotations in a review.

Cover art: "The Cosmic Dream Map" by Alison Chase Radcliffe
Book layout: Barbara Shaw

ISBN 978-1-7322882-1-8

First Edition

Published by:
Pony One Dog Press
Suite 113
1613 Harvard Street, NW
Washington, DC 20009

Emergency Room

BY
Alan Britt

Pony One Dog Press
Washington, DC

EMERGENCY ROOM

ACKNOWLEDGMENTS

The poems (sometimes in earlier versions) in this book appeared in the following publications. Grateful acknowledgement is made to the editors of those publications:

Alien Buddha: "Two Poets"

American Mustard: "Day in the Life"

Angry Old Man: "Sesame Street Viagra"

Ann Arbor Review: "Henry V," "Lovers in the Same Room," "The Present Is the Future & the Future Is Now," and "Butterscotch Fire Department Blues"

Anti-Heroin Chic: "Pancakes"

The Bitter Oleander: "Alarm Before the Snooze" and "Black Wooly"

Clockwise Cat: "Jam"

The Cultural Journal: "Neruda Sings Whitman"

Cultural Weekly: "Beauty"

Culture Cult Magazine (India): "Not Today"

Dark Matter: A Journal of Speculative Writing: "Pterodactyl Future"

Dissident Voice: "Asleep at the Wheel"

Earthen Lamp Journal (India): "Neruda Sings Whitman"

Five2One: "All Because of You"

Futures Trading: "Brothers: 2050"

GloMag (India): "Bullet"

January Review: "Plato's Tractor," "Faith," "Evolution," "Down Memory Lane," and "Two Poets"

Levure Littéraire (France-USA-Germany): "Peace Signs" and "The Cruelest Month"

Mad Swirl: "Chance Encounter"

Medusa's Kitchen: "Torch," "Never Too Early for Halloween," "What's in a Name?," and "Thursday Night, Early June"

Midnight Lane Boutique: "Friday Night Blues"

v

Mused: BellaOnline Literary Review: "Strolling with Students the Glen Arboretum at Towson University"

New Mystics: "Dawn"

Nixes Mate Review: "Anniversary"

Osiris: "Listening to the Daisy Jopling Band," "Amy," and "Forgiveness"

The Otter: "Occupying Wall Street"

The Pangolin Review: "Walt Whitman & William Blake Had Tea, or Was It Coffee?"

The Paragon Journal: "Separation of Church & State"

The Peregrine Muse: "The Day Young Immanentists Met Hugh Fox"

Poetry Pacific (Canada): "Banana Republics"

The Quail Bell Magazine: "Gazing at a Book," "Big Bang," and "Aperitif"

Ragazine: "It's Not Over Till We Say It's Over"

Scarlet Leaf Review (Canada): "First Grinder Poem"

Skidrow Penthouse: "Stone Violins," "Transatlantic Crossing," and "Doomsday: 12/21/12"

The Song Is . . .: "Get Thee to a House of Repute"

Unlikely Stories Mark V: "Not Your Father's Oldsmobile"

Venus in Scorpio Poetry E-Zine (Canada): "Zen"

Zombie Logic Review: "Emergency Room," "That Blessed Day," "Listening to Some Exquisite Violin & Thinking of Michelangelo," "When You Think About It," "Postponing Suicide," and "When You Don't Think About It"

* * *

"Occupying Wall Street*" in Time of the Poet Republic*, Mbizo Chirasha, Editor/Publisher, Miombopublishing, Zimbabwe: June, 2020

"Doomsday: 12/21/12" appeared in *Ragazine*, Mike Foldes, Editor, "Special Features" to celebrate "Oasis: An Evening of Music and Poetry" in collaboration with Robert Rosado, Director, La Ruche Arts Contemporary Consortium (LRACC) at the Union City Museum of

EMERGENCY ROOM

Art/William V. Musto Cultural Center, Union City, NJ: May 10, 2014

* * *

"Neruda Sings Whitman" in *Alianza: 5 U.S. Poets in Ecuador* (bilingual anthology in English with Spanish translations by Ricardo Pérez-Salamero García, Alex Lima, Lilvia Soto, and María Teresa Azuara), Alan Britt, Editor, CypressBooks, Rio Rico, AZ: 2015

"Words of Wisdom" in *Poetry Leaves* [Waterford Township Public Library]: Liz Waun, Adult Services Librarian, Poems hung in trees throughout the month of May 2-31, 2020 and then in the *Poetry Leaves* paperback anthology: November 2020

* * *

"Violin Smoke" and "Winter" in *Violin Smoke*, English/Hungarian, (Translated into Hungarian by Paul Sohar), Zoltán Böszörményi, Publisher, Iradalmi Jelen Könyvek Editions, Budapest, Hungary: 2015

Appreciation to those who offered encouragement throughout the writing of this book: Steve Barfield, Alberto Blanco, Brooke Bognanni, Zoltán Böszörményi, Mary Beth Britt, Heath Brougher, Nilda Cepero, Flavia Cosma, Niza Fabre, Red Focks, Paula Gottschalk, Clarinda Harriss, Charles P. Hayes, Claude Morency, Roberta Crawford Morency, Dzvinia Orlowsky, Scott Thomas Outlar, José Rodeiro, Paul B. Roth, Silvia Scheibli, Steve Sleboda, and Paul Sohar.

Special gratitude to David Churchill for his patience and unerring support for this project.

vii

Contents

INTRODUCTION by David Churchill | xiii

(Part 1)

Separation of Church & State | 3
The Day Young Immanentists Met Hugh Fox | 4
Torch | 5
Never Too Early for Halloween | 6
Alarm Before the Snooze | 7
Pancakes | 8
Banana Republics | 10
Get Thee to a House of Repute | 11
Occupying Wall Street | 12
Sesame Street Viagra | 15
Plato's Tractor | 16
Stone Violins | 17

(Part 2)

Gazing at a Book | 21
Neruda Sings Whitman | 22
Faith | 23
Asleep at the Wheel | 24
All Because of You | 26
Not Your Father's Oldsmobile | 27
Evolution | 28
Transatlantic Crossing | 29
Words of Wisdom | 33
It's Not Over Till We Say It's Over | 34

ALAN BRITT

Peace Signs | 36
Walt Whitman & William Blake Had Tea, or Was It Coffee? | 38
Emergency Room | 39
Doomsday: 12/21/12 | 41

(Part 3)

That Blessed Day | 45
What's in a Name? | 46
Henry V | 47
Listening to the Daisy Jopling Band | 48
Listening to Some Exquisite Violin & Thinking of Michelangelo | 49
When You Think About It | 50
Postponing Suicide | 51
When You Don't Think About It | 52
Lovers in the Same Room | 53
Big Bang | 54
Jam | 55
Amy | 56

(Part 4)

Dawn | 59
Day in the Life | 60
Forgiveness | 61
Aperitif | 62
Thursday Night, Early June | 63
Chance Encounter | 54
First Grinder Poem | 65
Down Memory Lane | 67
Zen | 68

EMERGENCY ROOM

Strolling with Students the Glen Arboretum at Towson University | 69
Beauty | 70
Bullet | 71
Brothers: 2050 | 72

(Part 5)

Black Wooly | 75
The Present Is the Future & the Future Is Now | 76
Butterscotch Fire Department Blues | 77
Anniversary | 78
Friday Night Blues | 79
Two Poets | 81
Not Today | 82
Transformation | 83
Winter | 85
Violin Smoke | 86
Pterodactyl Future | 87
The Cruelest Month | 88

Notes | 90

About the Author | 92

Publications | 93

EMERGENCY ROOM

Introduction

A QUESTION RAISED early in an interview with Alan Britt that appeared in the *Schuykill Valley Journal*, (you can find it reprinted in Britt's recent poetry collection *Dream Highway*), is an excellent place to begin this introduction. In that interview, the interviewer, Mark Danowsky, after first remarking on the social consciousness that comes through in so many of Britt's poems, remarks, "Maybe the more general question is really how you address 'big issues' without being didactic . . . "

Poets will recognize this as a challenge. How to stretch the artistic style to accommodate critical issues, without turning the poem into a mere teaching tool. Poems live for their readers because their meanings are amenable to being understood in different ways, not nailed down to the page. Readers don't want to be told what to think, even by the poet. Britt's 20th book of poetry, *Emergency Room*, a collection of what could be called some of his most profound and difficult work to date, offers us an example of how a poet addresses social issues without being didactic.

For the "issue" that underlies the *Emergency Room*, taken as a whole, is nothing less than America's descent into the twenty-first century's version of The Waste Land. Yet nothing in this collection could be called "didactic." The style is Britt's characteristic lyric, each poem with its own imagery and meaning. The more one reads, however, lulled perhaps by the artistic merit of each poem taken by itself, the more the poems as a whole weave together like leaves on a trellis, until one realizes that what one had taken for "leaves" may really have been the reticulated skin of a coiling python.

The effect is impressive. The sense of impending doom is greatly enhanced by being hidden. Britt's style acts as a form of misdirection. Think of the Shakespearean convention of moving the blood-letting off-stage. Often Britt's most trenchant observations are disguised in the most

xiii

recondite of images, as in this description of sentinel species from "Asleep at the Wheel":

> first to arrive were the most sensitive
> animals of the forest—painted bunting,
> lazy loris, & naked ani, a bird so tiny
> it must be inhaled like a gnat . . .

Could there be a more subtle image of an impending extinction than listing the animals affected first, without comment? It is akin to a murderer scrawling ERAWEB on his victim's mirror before killing him: the warning must be read more than once to be understood.

Your take on these poems—indeed on the collection as a whole—may be different from mine. I do encourage you to read the poems in order, though, from start to finish. The creative structure of the book is very precise. What follows then are some remarks that may serve as signposts of a sort, a few things I'd like to call to your attention as you go along, hopefully without prejudicing your own interpretations.

The First Poems

The first poem, "Separation of Church & State," asks the question: how long will it be before humans start acting humane? "So, how long will it be before we assist / those who are unable to assist themselves?" How long before humans, who are children of god, realize their true nature?

The second poem, "The Day Young Immanentists Met Hugh Fox," answers the question. It is not a good answer.

Best known for *Gods of the Cataclysm*, Fox has been described as a catastrophist, one of those who propose that it is only by catastrophe that progress occurs, as violent natural catastrophes have brought each of the world's geological ages to an end, resulting in mass extinctions across the globe, to be replaced by new forms. In *Gods of the Cataclysm*, Fox describes the Aztec myth of the four suns: one sun wiped out life on earth by wind, another by fire, still another by water, which he believed corresponded to Noah's flood. This last, he contends, was occasioned by a giant astral visitor that passed close to the earth, and was mistaken by ancient writers as the planet Venus.

The Immanentists refers to a group of college friends, including the speaker, who were inspired by European Surrealism and the idea of an indwelling spirit in each of us. The speaker and his friends fail to rebut Fox's theories. They fail to understand how the belief in a cataclysm could possibly contribute to the advent of the cataclysm itself. Here's how Fox, writing in *Gods of the Cataclysm*, imagines it:

> I was in a world in which the cosmos had gone insane. It wasn't just wind or even flood, but earthquakes ("land annihilating") the sun being covered over ("the bright light sent forth by the day…is withheld"), the whole order and symmetry of the world gone awry. I was back to the period of the Flood, the more-than-Flood, the time of the Great Cataclysm, the moment when the Celestial Visitor came into our solar system, creating huge tidal waves, wrenching open the surface of the earth, changing the alignment of the poles.

This, the poem seems to suggest, is what awaits us: no redemption for the human race till after the next cataclysm.

The last poem (a prose poem) in this trilogy provides a lyrical coda, in true Britt fashion, to this world-destroying vision as the speaker notices the "—shards of wings, / shattered antennae," of a dead beetle on his garage floor, who he imagines has tripped an IED provided by the forces of America's corporate powers. The speaker seems to put himself and his fellow Immanentists in the place of the beetle when he writes:

> …but all beetle wants is the truth, unspun by trained spinners, paid liars, & prostitutes of the cross. All he wants is one single drop of truth, one shimmering photon, one strand of DNA that stayed out late & met the ghost of Christmas Future.

Taken together, these three poems announce the collection's theme and establish its dimensions.

The Emergency Room

Two poems in the middle of the collection, "Emergency Room" and "Doomsday 12/21/12," describe what I take to be the same visit. In both cases the poems appear to be set during the Christmas holiday season (in fact, the date 12/21/12 is the winter solstice.) I believe this is a clue to the meaning of the Emergency room.

During the "unconscious" section described in "Emergency Room" (more on the unconscious section later), the speaker experiences "…nurse straightening *Newsweek* & *People* on plywood shelves near plastic spruce dripping raspberry gauze, golden cones, bright green bows & blinking white lights…" And again in "Doomsday: 12/21/12, ""Christmas tree with red gauze, golden cones, / & blinking white lights hissing like a possum."

An emergency room is a place where people go when they are in crisis. Here, with Christmas decorations on display, I believe one can argue that the emergency room represents Christianity. For two thousand years Christianity has been the place where people sought healing and solace. But America's Christianity has failed. As the speaker experiences, again in his unconscious state (more on this later), we see how Christianity itself has lost its way.

> … young wanderers…smiles like crucifixes like revolving
> doors & saints with hoodies like emerald EXIT sign's red
> arrow *pointing toward heaven up down east west in-between*
> … (Italics mine.)

And again:

> …a televangelist soliciting funds in the form of death bed
> confessions & beehive hairdo crushed beneath eighteen-
> wheeler tailgate (head lopped cantaloupe clean into Benz

backseat) as chuckling televangelist & squirming blond wig
on straw-colored microfiber sofa beside a plastic palm's
curved beak shimmering . . .

So much for the concern of a representative of American Christianity's
for a victim of a horrific traffic accident!

The Last Poems
The last two poems, "Pterodactyl Future" and "The Cruelest Month,"
bring the collection to a close that is neither hopeful nor despairing. But
it is an honest close, comforting nevertheless in its simplicity.

"Pterodactyl Future" is the speaker's answer to Hugh Fox's looked-
for next catastrophe. It's first (and last stanza) deserve to be quoted in
full:

> Pterodactyl claw of pollen singes
> my eyelash, sends a quiver to my
> mammalian brain that rain
> or some other meteorological
> phenomenon is a matter of faith
> & not my model for the future.

This simple statement, "not my model for the future," is all that can be
said, but coming as it does at the end of a collection where every other
line of "misdirecting" poetry is loaded with hidden meaning, this unas-
suming asseveration, almost like a line of plainsong, lays bare the re-
silience of at least this one speaker, and through him, mankind as a
whole. Perhaps the simplest in the whole collection, the lines in this
stanza are yet the most meaningful. The last line seems to come alive as
both a call to action and a promise.

By now no one should be surprised that the title of the very last
poem echoes the first line of T.S. Eliot's *The Waste Land*: "April is the
cruellest month." Though its meaning like the other poems is also am-

biguous, leading us into the national trauma that was Vietnam, one line, repeated several times, stands out for me: "a hand a torch." Harking back as it does to the joyful crooning of the "beetle" from the third poem in the collection, "Torch," here in the paddies of Vietnam calls to mind the rescuing hands of medics from " . . . Red Cross helicopters / like dragon flies hovering the paddies / flattened into jade salvation, into grey hairs sallowing cheekbones, / until a hand is a torch." This, another simple honesty, tells me that our survival as a species seems to lie in our connectedness.

A Note on the Use of Typographical Symbols
I have already called your attention to the first line of symbols that appear in the poem "Emergency Room." Though not the first occurrence of symbols in the collection, it's a good place to illustrate at least one of the uses to which the speaker puts them. Thus:
Like blotches of ink buzzards litter a stubble cornfield

The "blotches of ink buzzards" suggests the patient, or speaker, has begun seeing spots. The line of symbols then indicates the speaker has passed out. As the speaker is now unconscious, the symbols convey a state beyond words' ability to describe. The rest of the poem records the impressions the speaker receives: sounds, snatches of conversation, half-glimpsed images, in his subliminal state, where what is real mingles with the contents of his psyche in a dream-like fugue. (I leave it to the reader to decide for his or herself whether or not the speaker regains consciousness.) In other places the symbols seem to perform the function of an alphabet beyond words, an expanded form of punctuation as well as a menu of diacritical marks.

Hopefully these guideposts will help you as you enjoy the individual offerings and find your own meaning in them. I have endeavored to show how even a cursory reading of these select poems reveals enough of the theme to construct an outline of the whole, especially when read in order. So much more could be said about these poems of course but nothing in any of them comes across as didactic. Serious poets will turn to this book as an example of how to handle contemporary issues without compromising style or voice. The theme is built up poem by poem and line by line through an accumulating body of allusions, metaphors and subtleties. Once understood in their entirety, the poems take on deeper and even more subtle meanings when read in the light of the whole, fleshing out and offering their own commentary on the problem. This is a book that will be read, enjoyed and studied far into the future.

David B Churchill
June 15, 2021

1

These poems . . . correspond to my new spiritualist manner, pure disembodied emotion, detached from the control of logic, but note carefully, carefully, with a tremendous poetic logic. It is not surrealism, note carefully; the clearest consciousness illumines them.

–Federico García Lorca
(from a letter translated by Christopher Sawyer Lauçanno)

EMERGENCY ROOM

SEPARATION OF CHURCH & STATE

(La sublime mére du vinaigre . . .)
–Jacques Dupin

"Was Jesus a child of God?" asked
Crabb Robinson to William Blake
during one of their zany theological
discussions.

"Yes, he was. For that matter, so am I,
so are you, & Mary Magdalene as well,"
Billy advised Crabb, inserting a metaphysical
splinter into their ale-infested fantasies
leapfrogging the fiery hoops of one woman
in sequin bodysuit with hammers
in her hips smashing archaic love affairs.

Then, again, feral sax wails & crooner
croons that woman is slave to the slave
& only after a bipolar vortex curls its white
knuckles around the turquoise arteries
of hope, yikes, suffocating fate.

So, how long will it be before we assist
those who are unable to assist themselves?

ALAN BRITT

THE DAY YOUNG IMMANENTISTS MET HUGH FOX

We carried Hugh to our Del Rio apartment,
#208, or thereabouts, & offered him the only
piece of cushioned furniture we could afford,
then popped corn till wooly lambs
littered our psychedelic shag.

Hugh, like a rooster patrolling crickets,
plucked first one stray kernel, then another,
another, & so on.

No way we'd challenge this Michigan king—

But Hugh didn't miss a beat as he detailed
the shadowy lives of South & Central Americans
living on the margins.

We paddled the Blue Danube, a la *2001*, as Hugh
discussed *Ghost Dance*, *The Living Underground*,
& other visions for the American good.

Fox with jokes that cracked walnut shells while
juggling Jupiter moons like puppets on a string.

Hugh was Hugh, through & through.

EMERGENCY ROOM

TORCH

There was this beetle, cedar wings hunkered below a concrete step
for the short haul, minding his business, before tapping, I hazard,
tapping an IED. Guess what happened—shards of wings, shattered
antennae, plus a transmitter discarded by the Dumont Corporation—
before they sold Jackie, they pawned Babe for a minor fortune—
but those days are passé.

An aluminum ladder, beside an oil-stained garage floor tarpaulin,
prepares to escort beetle beyond his dilemma, but all beetle wants
is the truth, unspun by trained spinners, paid liars, & prostitutes
of the cross. All he wants is one single drop of truth, one shimmering
photon, one strand of DNA that stayed out late & met the ghost
of Christmas Future.

Be that as it may, beetle began crooning, crooning his ass off, panting
for all his worth, until one feathery sunrise resembling roseate spoonbills
ignited beetle's dreaming wings. You could've lit a torch that dawn.
I saw it but didn't light up. No, sir. Not anymore.

5

ALAN BRITT

NEVER TOO EARLY FOR HALLOWEEN

Mask of the walrus curdles your blood
while fumbling for icebergs resembling
shards of Styrofoam huddling corals
& coiling mangroves shin deep around
a tropical disturbance whose name is long
forgotten, though, I tracked her, '65, the
year of *Help*, the year of napalm, the year
we embraced the years, then subsequently
became orphans for goblins steeping our
astrological algorithms & frothing our
coffees with decaffeinated dreams.

EMERGENCY ROOM

ALARM BEFORE THE SNOOZE

(After the *Three Little Pigs*)

I was devastated, then the salvage truck
arrived—inside-out I wondered if I could
spend the night dreaming a wild century
of virgin crocuses appearing behind me
while occupying boring daylight beside
myself, just to exude faith, just to exhume
all the tricky bastards who've elbowed their
way into history books, expressways, &
holidays named after, plus retirements to
die for, their plan, to celebrate the cemeteries
we supported last session, plus the one
before that, then there's that nasty medical
condition no one admits to, kitten rescued
from a drainpipe the size of bubblegum, bits
of this, bits of that, bits of bits, rat-infested
bits, & bits that roam the flesh; we call them
many names, too many to mention, but
many names is a mercenary capable of crushing
the marble columns of the union—till then
the zeitgeist hunkered between these bits
better seal our straw temples together
long after they come looking for us.

PANCAKES

Plaster eyes, indentations
like mascara penumbras
sent to deify the Pharaoh.

Cherubs, zygote angels, deliver slices
of wheat berry, sans gluten.

Arizona jaguar rippling a Liszt piano
licks its saffron nose & yawns a rainbow
of silk geishas crossing the border.

Priest's bloodstained robe,
as priests' robes
often hint of tarnished iron,
lodges teeth into vertebrae
out of habit, dressed in habit,
& slashes a gaseous mountain
large enough,
large enough to shield bald eagles,
heretic cougars, & rusty grizzlies,
plus sawdust sunlight showering
an upper 16th century row house's
afternoon milkmaid hiding the affair
beneath layers of consternation & silk.

EMERGENCY ROOM

Puerto, Puerto, Rico, Rico.

Puerto the firefly blasting his way
through the universe knows the secret,
secret of liquorice religion,
secret to secret's secrets
that plunged roots long ago through the garlic tidal,
wild onion, & toxic copper from Neruda's grave.

Silk adjectives stained by wine kisses
weave a lace of white lightning
on bended knee, begging for mercy,
& solemn to religion the way lightning
shivers the August air we breathe
& piss in—right after that your family
reunion could be my family reunion,
& you know what that means.

BANANA REPUBLICS

Flax seed, one worthy of Jupiter's
carpenter blue light.

Nickel coin, hole drilled thru copper skull.

Dehydrated verbs & adjectives like
onions dying to be caramelized.

Groundhog bloodies its teeth
against 14-gauge galvanized steel,
blueberry blue, positive there
is no afterlife.

Ah, but the US & its nonprofit ruse,
posing Fidel as a cottonmouth
along the Intracoastal near Ft. Myers
& nestled between the overthrow
of Guatemala circa Eisenhower,
or El Salvador or Chile, circa who
gives a flying fuck, circa who gives
one, anyway?

EMERGENCY ROOM

GET THEE TO A HOUSE OF REPUTE

Boardwalk model's twisted seaweed quaff—
jade dragon tattooing her lower back
as spandex jiggles adventurous avocados
inside one's fecund imagination.

I worshipped an Anglo-Saxon toothless
monarch eons ago & watched his Danish
cousin lift her muddy skirt for a border guard
during one particularly gruesome occupation.

That Danish cousin be damned—I couldn't
help but help myself, so I dove headlong
into her ultramarine & canary-speckled eyes
with nary a thought of looking back!

ALAN BRITT

OCCUPYING WALL STREET

> (*And what would Karen Silkwood say to you,
> I mean if she was still alive?*)
> —Gil Scott-Heron

Fed flanked by elected officials
enters a bank, canvas bag & Glock
cocked with insane rounds.

White tombstones.

Sulfur wind through skeleton elms
& moonlight like crushed roach tablets
across the buttocks of the vicar
in charge of potluck luncheons,
in charge of elections, in charge
of those in charge of nothing. That
hurts: charged for nothing in return,
charged for being charged for following,
charged for snapping elbows
& wishbones for the Inquisition, charged
for grievances between cheetah &
zebra stallion shattering vocal cords
with one intellectual hoof, charged
for falling in love, charged for being
there, charged for not being there,
charged for flying too close,
charged for being in the right place
at the wrong time (karma),
charged for being charged, charged
for daydreaming pomegranate
tentacles for fantasy fish 12 miles

EMERGENCY ROOM

below sunlight, charged for allowing
oneself to be charged (see Fred Douglass),
charged for the ocean, charged for Neptune's rings,
charged for ashes in the eyes of immigrant
grandmothers & daughters on the verge
of committing themselves before they're
ready, years before bridges constructed
by desperate #2 for the hierarchy,
toxic mind & years before there were years,
so many years before that.

Across the ceiling a two-way uncoils
then unbuttons her blouse for humanity
after a session with confession, after top lip
smudges bottom lip to lop-side both lips
pulsating cocaine onto a tongue that chose
the life of a heretic rather than quiver
in the garden like a tuxedo cat named
Lilith with eyes of avocado knives
slicing white shadows from the years
between us, years between hand-cranked
pumps of the heart during drought,
during dreams of droughts, during a drought
of dreams dreaming that droughts appear
without warning from a magician's top hat
as a leopard print bikini juggles your balls
across the river that Moses restored to sanity,
across the Delaware & Delaware's insidious tolls,
across synapses dislocated by traditional lightning

ALAN BRITT

flinched from Texas floods made from cellphones
dangling a cask of amontillado or cashmere
squirting juices through stained-glass fingernails,
across the tundra that shivers the shingles
from each house housing two dogs & two children,
I say two dogs & the children our children bring
to the table sans futures & real estate gone viral,
no longer Conestoga, no longer remotely close
to what those who perished in '76 stood for.

EMERGENCY ROOM

SESAME STREET VIAGRA

Good for what ails you.

Dysfunction at the junction.

ALAN BRITT

PLATO'S TRACTOR

At 11:11 roses melting gasoline tank beside a cane rocker frosted with thunder clouds & hydrogen beyond recognition→"Although," she mused, "what spewed from incinerator stacks resembled congressmen & was nothing like purported, even though," she lamented "their eyelids were wooden shutters caved completely in."→→Typical diatribe, I thought, but worth the wait→→→Below her withers lurked an angel made of a conch shell's swirling faith that everything's on fire with voices consisting of tarpaper & mud nestled into coral kitchens chirping for bamboo like cobras leaping from stainless steel faucets & arcing like blue flying fish with switchblade fins sailing over the Atlantic→→→→like ambulance screams, like icicle eyelashes, like bolts of lightning with tarpon scales the size of lazy thoughts steaming, billowing, flickering from a brahma skull leaning against a barn set ablaze by a metabolic moon & doused by roses leaking from the empty tank on a red tractor or the shadow of a red tractor→→→→→whichever comes first.

EMERGENCY ROOM

STONE VIOLINS

The stone violins were nothing more
than an aborted attempt.

Whoever heard of music
made of stone
anyway?

After all, poems encouraged
canine companionship, so I endured
rotary telephones, sirens, & dozen-year-old
bug lights slurping humid darkness.

One learns
humility from a dog more easily
than from a human.

Dogs observe with eyes
that say *I can't go on—*
so is
it
any wonder
some humans prefer the deep rings,
the bloody centers
of
hibiscus aureoles
over dreams that abandon them
beneath bridges
above the unaffordable YMCA?

ALAN BRITT

When Butler Road flinches, a red fox
      devours headlights & glances
  forth & back before traversing stony darkness.

    Ecdysis: I shed my skin.

    Mercurial wind
        arrives
   on the blazing horns
of a leopard slug's ———Ψ———●→→→ muscular tongue
    just as cotton
     drawstrings
      crumple
      to
      the
      floor
       of
      varnished
       maple.

2

If our species is to survive, we must embrace what makes us unique as well as what makes us universal.

–Marsh River, greatest Abyssinian cat to grace the townhouse of El Alambre

GAZING AT A BOOK

Curled fairytales.

Federico dangling
Franco puppets
with entrails
exploding
party favors
from the barrels
of German Mausers.

Bull enters with candles
for horns.

Too bad the moon
has a tainted reputation;
too bad both families
ingested dynamite;
too bad scum
rises
to the top.

Too bad.

ALAN BRITT

NERUDA SINGS WHITMAN

It was like the invisible salt of waves,
you said, when you were just about
an internal combustion me. Back when
you had lots of heart & some dark energy,
you said pinch the head off Ozymandias,
so poor folks could get their fill,
& fill they did, for a moment, until
United Fruit snatched it away again.

You named the names required of truth.

Alternative?

If now I believe in dark energy, & there
seems to be good evidence for it, then
surely I believe in you, Pablo, son of Walt,
incomparable poet of love & mischief.

EMERGENCY ROOM

FAITH

Sling blue.

Wishful.

Ludwig's "Great Fugue,"
like it was written for his mother.

Teddy bear, cotton rag,
boyhood fascination
requiring APA response—
nothing but APA sizzles upper
thighs into stainless affairs
across executive desks—neckties
askew, creased Pima cotton, top button
AWOL, bussing lips like scorpions—
tomorrow's another day.

ALAN BRITT

ASLEEP AT THE WHEEL

Brass clouds, atoms gone
viral, beyond god control,
atoms believing they lead unique lives.

Brass clouds of atoms like wasps
pay close attention to those
they refuse to bury under any circumstance,
like marrow,
like those likely to impersonate
icons as, say, totems that zest
temporary spoils
over every sleight-of-hand grenade
exchanged for a wheelchair.

Mescaline eyelashes pump
a toothpick crowd teething
bites from sterling parchment trays:
blended cheeses, feral ham
on baked chips
of two or more orgasmic
Midwestern ingredients; shame on amphibians;
T. rex arose 4 am sharp
beyond the tar pits of La Brea—
producers first to mobilize,
cellphones twinkling pitch black limousines,
fathers disappearing down ant lion quicksand—
first to arrive were the most sensitive
animals of the forest—painted bunting,
lazy loris, & naked ani, a bird so tiny

EMERGENCY ROOM

it must be inhaled like a gnat
(speck with wings) or filament woven
into a moral curtain—philosophical curtain,
curtain tasting of hammers & rusted supervision,
curtain smelted into iron by negligence,
by falling asleep at the wheel,
by agreeing to everything
& power napping the apex
of our on-going crisis.

ALAN BRITT

ALL BECAUSE OF YOU
(After U2)

Dawn full of blades.

Membrane of sleep
separates us
from vegetation's
neural aberration—atoms
overheated & spawning gills
in the face of annihilation,
toucan beaks stabbing
all the god-damned bananas,
goldenrod melon, sea foam cantaloupe,
& life rafts after captain & crew
absconded, cocktail tables listing,
string fantasy like champagne fizz,
knees soaked in doubt, & walls
made from balsa architecture
too weak to withstand
all the radiated
emails from oblivion.

EMERGENCY ROOM

NOT YOUR FATHER'S OLDSMOBILE

Not tonight.

Not now.

Brain off the hook.

Sense of beings
stalled at carwashes,
spiritual drive-thrus,
so slam the lid
on steam rising
from Sunday
morning dreams
swirling neon insinuations
of the men or women
we long to be
while forgetting
for one nano that
we're precisely
the men & women
we're supposed to be.

ALAN BRITT

EVOLUTION

Tax imaginations—as one expects
to gain from such folly—but there's
a dark side.

Always dark when lost in the Black
Forest of neurons minding someone
else's business, someone else's prime
of life like saints enjoying oral
sex with nuns, plus philosophers
on the fringe of intelligence,
intelligence, I say, suspenders, fine,
but quasi-divine support of whatever
existential notion bobs its nose
like a Peruvian turtle with banana stripes
from onyx cheek to barber pole neck
that says this swamp, this earthly heaven
is all I know. True, I haven't launched
satellites, & I haven't stretched cable
port to port, but there's one thing,
god, known by many as evolution,
DNA, survival—he/she/it goes by
many names—one thing's certain:
my shell, this thing that protects me
from you & worships a frog in estrous
shedding ten quadrillion ampules
of eggs before her one trillion lovers
if nothing else has taught me,
in short, to grow the fuck up!

EMERGENCY ROOM

TRANSATLANTIC CROSSING

Transporting anything across the mother waters
is dangerous. We live with that.

But not crossing . . . tantamount to everything else.

So, we load tapestries onto steamers & antigravity
luxury liners like roughage through the bowels
of early 21st century.

Could be better;
could be worse.

Like Bartok said,
someone's asleep at the cosmic wheel
while others merely dream
of being asleep.

Like Francisco Goya
pulling black tapeworms from our psyches
or Hieronymus Bosch, Hieronymus the magnificent,
most underrated of all,
H.B. to you & me,
but Boschy whose brush was a razor
of magical invention,
Medieval angst like algae
nibbling our medulla oblongata
as the tides roll in & out. Morals
shift, the Drift sways & those

ALAN BRITT

in lockjaw pretend to understand_o

o

o

o

O O o O O

submerged

to

the

gills

with

invest

mints

gone

awry.

Still pomegranate, lavender & silk promises

burning

l

i

k

e

a

California

l

i   d

w   f

i

r

e

EMERGENCY ROOM

through
the populace
of Count Vlad's
damaged
br

a

in

cells
or Khan's vision of divine providence.

★

Sky filled with spiny
starfish
or mullet
flopping
Lake Worth's warped moonlit pier;
joy   like   fishing
line
tangled,   joy   like   monofilament
indiscretion,
alchemical
malcontent.

★   ★

Anyway, tugs were sweeping
the last

ALAN BRITT

UFO's
    from
        green
            radar
with ads of lip gloss, hair shiners,
  &   cars   guaranteed
    to   drive   you
    f u r t h e r   i n t o
    d   e   b   t
  than   you   ever
    thought
    p o s s i b l e .

N e v e r m o r e . N e v e r b e f o r e .
N e v e r b e f o r e
&
n e v e r
a g a i n,
notonemore
godforsaken
minute,
never,
I
say,
no
more
fuel
left
for
lies.

WORDS OF WISDOM

Words don't kill us. They
make us stronger.

I know, it's harder to talk
than to shoot, but we
have to do it.

For the sake of the babies.

For the sake of everything.

ALAN BRITT

IT'S NOT OVER TILL WE SAY IT'S OVER

That's why they're called safety matches;
duck your head before striking.

That's when the tarnished Indian elephant coin
bank with iron-stripped flathead screw divorced
both ribcages spilling wheat pennies, buffaloes,
Mercury dimes, & quarters in diaphanous Victorian
gowns to flow across knuckles resembling two
golden drops of sensible venom.

Looks like your liver's doing fine,
says Humboldt to the lobster, chops
held in check by OCD anniversary
over shellfish shaved ice buffets,
(Easter or Mother's Day), shoes
abandoned beside the creek where
fallen logs resemble small gators trolling
inner tubes beside cardboard boxes
face down, corporate tattoos blurred.

8

I turn around, when I can,
I turn to look
where I've been.

EMERGENCY ROOM

I turn, according to yoga,
according to linguistic pretzel dreams
steeped in alchemical verbs, nouns & adjectives,
with interjections & careless conjunctions
tossing Mardi Gras beads to bare-chested
prepositions pilfering fast-food dumpsters
& haunting merlot eyelashes to spot a fry
below lusty chicken leg busted in three
places, but a fry, & just when we thought!

ALAN BRITT

PEACE SIGNS

    (Thanks, John)

Uptight, short-sighted, narrow-minded hypocrites
twisting their hands beneath every New Age dryer
in every Cracker Barrel men's room.

(Aluminum handle devastates.)

Corkboard's lonely thumbtacks journey
from smile to gloom during one semester
while stoned G & drunken A waltz around
the pool naked as god intended before sifting
toes beneath the sands of San Paolo
the moment a poet keels over granite
kitchen isle while slicing August tomatoes,
cukes, & yellow peppers to make the Redcoats
blush→→→→→→→→→hygiene
just the same.

↓ ↓ ↓ ↓ ↓ ↓ ↓ ↓ ↓ ↓ ↓ ↓ ↓ ↓

Guitar notes like dirty egrets off Fort Myers,
heat lightning, notes like ochre extracted
from Gilas & transferred through fingertips
bleating like lambs at slaughter 16 paces
before the Tyger says, *I'm worth every dime, &*
so are you, that said, that said, that bled, that bled.

⚦ + ⚨ = ♥ ⚨ ⚦ ☠ ☮

EMERGENCY ROOM

They used pitchforks for guitars; each
tong sharpened to perfection, at which
point the designated Thomson's gazelle,
spindly creature, cinnamon back, shoe polish
tears, & cotton belly, suddenly decides
to become a harmonica today, since no one,
as Federico lamented not so long ago,
wishes to be a harmonica!

Yet, there it is.

[Opening italics by John Lennon]

ALAN BRITT

WALT WHITMAN & WILLIAM BLAKE HAD TEA, OR WAS IT COFFEE?

Floor polisher swirls clouds resembling a flock of sheep from 1817 outside London, a tenor breeches a Brooklyn tenement, a grasshopper made of ink twitches for its mate before dodging a murmuration of starlings shapeshifting above Glyndon Avenue—but the more Crabb huffed & puffed, the bolder Blake became on issues tasting like lamb on a spit, garlic salted, & country buttered to perfection— you couldn't break him loose with a hickory stick, & you can't get rid of him, so, what the hell, why not embrace him.

EMERGENCY ROOM

Ocean creeps through soda machine's heated gills

Blood pressure: 79/49

White-haired wheelchair in purple knits

Cinnamon nylons puddled like rubber bands around swollen ankles

Fox 45 visits Newtown, Connecticut

Back pain's piranha . . . lower vertebrae

Severe cough's traffic jam on northbound 95

Samsung flat screen's tractor trailer triple skids across Ohio I-80's black ice

Like blotches of ink buzzards litter a stubble cornfield

Feathers like ash like 60-round clips like adjectives crumpled into stainless steel cans like smartphones riding the white backs of stallions circling circus rings littered with sawdust hash tags & pulverized vertebrae like recessed light bulbs like an appendix sinking to the bottom of the Black Sea like nurse straightening *Newsweek* & *People* on plywood shelves near plastic spruce dripping raspberry gauze, golden cones, bright green bows, & blinking white lights tacked to walnut overlay like titanium thoughts like smoke in the shape of corroded angels like tongues in the shape of corroded smoke like eyeballs bouncing between metal jacks sprawled across rhino linoleum like voices left out in the rain, edges curled like stale bologna, voices wading marijuana fields' sticky red-veined ceremonial bulbs that taste like liquorice like young wanderers in seer sucker sun dresses faded baseball caps & smiles like crucifixes like revolving doors & saints with hoodies like emerald EXIT sign's red arrow pointing toward heaven up down east west in-between the onionskin layers separating one dimension from another like each electron aggravating each neutron & forcing each proton to reveal itself as giraffe or moose, emerald housefly in blazing estrous, ether masks covering the lips of holocausts, as orderly in paper slippers poaching a Pepsi from soda machine wheezing a televangelist soliciting funds in the form of death bed confessions & beehive hairdo crushed beneath eighteen-wheeler tailgate (head lopped cantaloupe clean into Benz backseat) as chuckling televangelist & squirming blond wig on straw-colored microfiber sofa beside a plastic palm's curved beak shimmering a snack machine wheezing crackly bags of chips, nuts, candies, encased in twinkling white lights

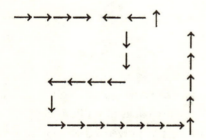

EMERGENCY ROOM

DOOMSDAY: 12/21/12

Bleached blonde, black eyebrows —

In case of fire break glass —

Emergency flashers recessed inside skull —

Bullfrog cello with sore throat —

Knocks at the door —

Paper gown removed, vitals checked —

Adjectives braided like scorpions —

Cellphone wheelchair —

Lies about love angry love —

Christmas tree with red gauze, golden cones,
        & blinking white lights hissing like a possum
        in darkest corner of coffin —

Small white dog with pink skin, cataract
        about to bloom —

Detroit gangs fake each other's deaths —

Greektown serves shell casings
        as steamed mussels for lunch —

Clouds of magnesium —

ALAN BRITT

Helium kisses —

Sunglasses the size of sunflowers —

Roman numeral X on wall clock leaps
to its death —

Raining mercury in Estonia —

Raining ashes in Cincinnati —

Raining bicycles in Berlin —

Raining gramophones in Bangladesh —

Raining mustaches in Pittsburgh —

Raining reindeer in Iraq —

Plastic roses at Italian bistros die
of liver cancer —

Snow plow scrapes electrons into
a cocaine parking lot —

Drones in your shower, drones in your
underwear, drones in your anus —

Just saying —

3

Perhaps one of the greatest flaws of humanity is that one has to be reminded constantly of one's humility, but these constant reminders, if one acknowledges them, have the power to effect great change.

–Sean Frederick Forbes

EMERGENCY ROOM

THAT BLESSED DAY

If I found myself in Shakespeare's company
cruising the thermals high above a tarnished
sterling platter of mantis celery, white cheeses
harpooned by bruised dandelion & aborted
raspberry cellophane toothpicks, plus jaundiced
dips speckled with flea-sized spices, I'd bow
before Sir William (or the Earl) & apologize
for scorpions prowling the perimeter of my
recent indigestion, thereby expunging all
previous regrets from my periodic battles
with academic seizures.

ALAN BRITT

WHAT'S IN A NAME?

Richard the Lionheart to Richard the II, followed
by scoliosis the III, then a succession of Henrys.

Like soccer affiliations these bloodlines of Jameses
& Georges forged alliances into genocidal namesakes
long before tropical disturbances littered a necklace
of coconuts across the concrete throat of a West
Palm curb one day, 1956, or so, thus excreting
the latest zeitgeist from the clogged
gold-plated bowels of the kings.

How sad.

EMERGENCY ROOM

HENRY V

> (*The more we tolerate, the better our poetry.*)
> –Wm. Shakespeare Jones

So says he. So says the one nurtured
by early moons when the sun was liquid;
so says my father & yours. Which poses a dialectic
dilemma: Must we only weep manna that we
cannot taste, touch or smell, so foreign to God?

So says the reverse of he, & so says the other.

In words that my father & yours never spoke,
imagine a horse, a feral horse beneath the moon's
liquid vibrations commencing to grind our nucleus
into, dare I say, a midsummer night's dream or
something that tastes just the way we like it.

ALAN BRITT

LISTENING TO THE DAISY JOPLING BAND

Volcanoes usurp Mars, moons lift their skirts
to avoid 16th century myths encased in ice—
cougar violin shakes her filthy nape, then absconds
with family shepherd into the exotic blue haze
beyond another rubber band day at the office.

I sit, violin strings 200° minus zero→ →bow's
mossy antlers with Saxon eyes, blonde scorpion
tail, praying mantis wings rolled like Cubans
beneath a dream of red-tailed hawks rustling
the bloody ashes of dawn.

EMERGENCY ROOM

LISTENING TO SOME EXQUISITE VIOLIN
& THINKING OF MICHELANGELO

(After Daisy Jopling)

Mantis eyes flicker gas blue flames—
barefoot verb pirouettes scalding ice—
disturbance of coconuts waist deep &
bare-chested into the lake that Michelangelo
enjoyed as a boy on full moons, yet flames
prowl the golden thicket like mother otter
with infants in tow as heat wave melts terracotta
tiles over an algae-coated Beverly Hills chateau—
"Hi, I'm Michelangelo, be sure to tip the mice
who shoulder ice from the whitewashed shed
& tell 'em that cheeses are on the house,
wherever that house shall be!"

ALAN BRITT

WHEN YOU THINK ABOUT IT

Frustrated, first one picks up a rock,
second one, petrified timber, third one
wanders gloriously drunk through the electric
blue forest of Austria, while the fourth one
kicks his Ludwig igniting the most dynamic
rock 'n' roll quartet in history.

We circled the moon's waist on a raft
of driftwood across a sea of blood.

WWII left its mark on us—so now we'll
never go quietly or any other crazy adverb
into this or that godforsaken night someday.

But we've got rhythm, plenty of rhythm.

EMERGENCY ROOM

POSTPONING SUICIDE

If you thought folks chose suicide
over a backyard bug zapper's blue
sparks splintering canasta, pinochle,
& fat cigar lotus clouds swirling
the local morgue was a perfect crock
of shit, then you weren't paying
much attention.

Me, either.

But, think about it—before the
bank jams alleyways, clogs arteries
called ports, & coerces reluctant
restaurateurs, in long run or the short,
because it's better that way.

ALAN BRITT

WHEN YOU DON'T THINK ABOUT IT

It makes sense: we age, we bore with vagaries
twisting tall tales because the truth is too expensive,
so we quilt the Lord's Prayer on a niece's christening
blanket—chop confessions into firewood—lest we
find ourselves at the end of a long journey from stars
sprawled like octopi 200 feet across a minute or
a day, if, for example, the Pope suddenly, inexplicably,
retires to 300 acres of prime pasture, thanks to you
& me.

Make sense?

LOVERS IN THE SAME ROOM

> (Before Francis)

Two bananas, exhausted lovers,
reflect a crucifix across the glass
dome of a crockpot
where two adults with katydids
in their fingertips
& frankincense curling their chests
to say they've earned the right,
like geese, they've graduated
cosmetics, bank statements,
iPads, & Droids,
anxious evolutions,
or the lack thereof—
lovers like two bananas, Cuban style,
like two mildly bruised priests
escaping the confines
of the Vatican.

ALAN BRITT

BIG BANG

Faster than the speed of light—
the speed of birth.

That's what it takes
to overcome inertia,
to rise from disorganized dust
before fate derails
the entire process all over again.

So, before you blink an eye,
plus 50 trillion years before
considering to blink, add
another 17 quadrillion years
& you have a pretty good
idea what it takes
to emerge from chaos.

EMERGENCY ROOM

JAM

A journal called *Scorpion Lunch*,
or Jeff Beck jazzing,
glass tubing his Fender —
rusty-headed mermaid stumbles
into expectations, yet
.ooOOOOOoo.one senses the end
could be right around any given
corner at any proverbial moment,
so, why not trace his "Coy Mistress"
to "Approximate Man" or "Foam,"
as though a groaning cello gave this
young nymph permission to step
from a coconut rolled below a West
Palm curb, I don't know, 1956 or so,
like a gecko with lava-colored shoulders
inflamed by someone else's imagination
disturbing a jazz quintet that spawned
an anarchist British blues band stripped
naked beneath a stained-glass window
with quartz tears falling from heaven
before morphing into red-veined
sprouts from Amsterdam.

In the end, it comes down to lips,
black plum lips, lips stained
by enthusiasm, organic or otherwise,
lips that think a wild imagination
is the perfect meaning of life.

55

ALAN BRITT

AMY
(After Amy Winehouse)

She gave everything to the song—
not much left for life, life as most
folks squeeze their shutters
when stress overwhelms—she
gave the song everything.

She approached me.

We rolled miniature carts down
organic herb & vitamin aisles
designed for every ailment, & that's
where we fell in love—the place we
kissed in bank teller light with the
passion of two gnostic saints
buried chest deep in limestone.

4

*The best lack all conviction, while the worst
Are full of passionate intensity.*

–William Butler Yeats

EMERGENCY ROOM

DAWN

It's been decades, eons, 10,000 wonders
of the universe.

It's been death & rebirth, rebirth & death.

It's been since Pablo took that injection
like the superhero he was; it's been that
& much, much more.

More than we can bear;
that's how it seems.

It's been, *I don't believe we allowed that to happen.*
Where was punctum when we needed it the most?

It's been tomatoes weeping July thunderstorms;
it's been two trillion dreams splintered
by insurance companies into quantum logistics.

It's been Donne & Marvell, Blake & Coleridge,
Shelley & Keats; it's been hedges exploding
like grenades; it's been dry-rotting soffits
below aluminum gutters & robins assaulted
by midafternoon storm clouds.

It's been decades, eons, one trillion wonders
of the universe.

It's been death & rebirth, rebirth & death.

59

ALAN BRITT

DAY IN THE LIFE

Acting normal while they take us to war.

Acting like red maple's dried blood.

Acting like acting ever did us any good.

?   ?   ?   ?

Rain pounds magnolias.

Cucumber tendrils' lacy attitudes,
high fashion.

Pregnant 767 scours zero visibility.

∞   ∞   ∞   ∞

Slapping the carport with swordfish.

Cardinals compose a garnet duet
inside my straw-colored bones.

EMERGENCY ROOM

FORGIVENESS

My relationship with Daphne improves daily.

Golden ringlets & rust-stained knuckles.

Buick SUV hisses our side street.

Female cardinal carves her initials
into the pecan shoulder of dusk.

Japanese maple's bruised solitude.

Summer rain like Krupa pounding white Igloo®
cooler discarded by everyone & sent by everyone
to plug the ubiquitous black hole in my universe.

APERITIF

61º feels like a female cardinal
igniting dawn's brass eyelid.

61º smokes organic sweet death.

Roulette taunts jealous fate.

Dove's coo carves the quicksilver dusk.

Debussy oboe dons a waist of kerosene.

At 61º maples make love to magnolias.

EMERGENCY ROOM

THURSDAY NIGHT, EARLY JUNE

Working his brain to bits & farming too,
said the 6th grader who had to rhyme

but changed his mind just in thyme.
Said a rain-soaked garden hose, coiling

mass of garters. Said the cardinal appearing
two poems ago challenging a Poulenc catbird

whose chirrups resembled the sandpaper
screeches of drunken cicadas smearing

a tropical storm's gypsy mascara across
the wandering eyelids of dusk.

*   *   *

& that's how four goldenrod cucumber
trumpets embrace the anaconda rain!

ALAN BRITT

CHANCE ENCOUNTER

When she asks, *Would you like to seduce me?*,
I scissor her illusionist hips & say,
I live here, even though I'm passing through.

She folds four porcelain knuckles
beneath her chin & muses, *This universe
needs work. A slave is a slave is a slave is a slave
& time to abolish this ungodly nonsense.*

I agree & pursue what I came for: Quantum
lightning in every sector of my brain before
she fluffs her 4000-thread opalescent wing
& says, *I'm buried to my chest in sin. It'll take more
than guilty kisses to set me free. How about you?*

Not hearing well these days, I sprinkle organic
thoughts onto a skillet primed with extra virgin
cold pressed olive oil, Greek, & fresh sprigs
of Italian parsley, immune to the future.

EMERGENCY ROOM

FIRST GRINDER POEM

> (*Punish the monkey*
> *and let the organ grinder go.*)
> –Mark Knopfler

So it goes as long as grinders blend
souls into hypnotic servitude.

But, what if, suspend your Freudian
suspenders & grind like Rimbaud—
flash Laertes' blade fanning the flames
of melancholy & Arthur dreaming
of carbines, grind that junta tin
grinder weaving the salt of those
banished into atoms long before
preschool was an Easter egg hunt
for one faded tortoiseshell in a
sapling before stumbling upon
an adolescent nest of cracked
lavenders with tangerine swirls.

Grind like grinding is revered above
ice angels melting graves,
Albuquerque sunsets,
mother earth, & mustard coral
squished between the damage done
by whispering instead
of speaking our crazy minds.

ALAN BRITT

When did we abandon our minds,
& when will the Great Experiment
embroider a suspension bridge
across an existential existence
that won't scare the living shit
out of mothers & grandmothers?

[It's not what you think.]

EMERGENCY ROOM

DOWN MEMORY LANE

All those ancestors in the way
of rebirth,
clogging the pores
of evolution.

Damn them & me.

Damn them & me,
well, well, well, well—
love eyelines a moonlit canoe,
her mother-of-pearl atoms
popping like piranha hunting
for heartaches.

Well, I saw a sign made
of mercury & on that sign
your voice over & over
dusted like crabapple petals
littering a goldenrod school
bus's wooly caterpillar head.

So, how've you been
all these years?

ZEN

One minute mullets slap my face,
slash my grin, & fill the boat,
while next I'm chasing split fingers
in the dirt.

One minute folks beg photos
for basement mausoleums,
while next I'm coughing up steroids
in a walnut-paneled definition
of the Old Testament's Heaven & Hell.

One minute thunder plunders
my virgin hips of imagination,
while next I'm waltzing the existential
end off a short pier.

One minute I'm a saffron wasp
drilling the succulent spine
of a green leaf caterpillar hidden
beneath a July broccoli frond.

Unfortunately, he's the one!

EMERGENCY ROOM

STROLLING WITH STUDENTS THE GLEN ARBORETUM AT TOWSON UNIVERSITY

We wander as lemon shadows
past the holly's jade pearls
& below a waxy spruce's thick feathers,
past pine sweat oozing naked woodchips,
& blue obelisk's ivory lettering
that resembles melaleuca's peeling edges,
plus Dogwood's chameleon skin
with pear-shaped leaves backlit
to reveal ultramarine veins
across a newborn's skull

At my touch a beech tree's elephant
trunk flows chilly blood
through its medusa limbs

Infant mantis' one inch twig body
with four silk hind legs
& two spiderweb front legs
bent at the elbows

Oak roots flow like octopi—
squirrel perches upside down,
tail flattened against giant oak trunk,
lower jaw jutted beneath whiskers,
ears shaped like clover petals,
upper body curled like a question
mark against the glutted afternoon,
eyes of espresso beans

69

ALAN BRITT

BEAUTY

(*"Beauty is truth, truth beauty,"—that is all
Ye know on earth, and all ye need to know.*)
–John Keats

Yet, beauty terrifies. Some want to destroy it, want to stab, strangle, shoot & dispute it, undermine it, satirize it, sanitize it, spit on it, pock it with cigarette butts, terrorize it, smash it with a hammer, imprison it, incinerate it, outlaw it, ridicule it, shame it, ignore it, banish it, tax it, annihilate it, mutilate, sabotage, nuke & eradicate it, brutalize it, smash & deconstruct, debauch, torment, & demoralize it, subvert it, paralyze it, disgrace it, capitalize & crush it, harass it, prosecute, drown & cauterize it, defame, pollute & humiliate it, scandalize, ravage & shatter it, slander it, stigmatize & debase it, disfigure, denigrate & molest it, electrocute & incarcerate it forever, which makes it sound so damned close to the truth—have we forgotten what truth looks like? Then perhaps it's time to flaunt paisley sundresses & tie-dyed t-shirts designed by shamans strumming sitars to inspire a basic mistrust of faux philosophers in Kevlar vests who disallow imagination to flow the way it did before we feared it might never flow that way again.

EMERGENCY ROOM

BULLET

If you wash a bullet
beneath the waterfall
of empathy,
it'll never
leave its chamber.

ALAN BRITT

BROTHERS: 2050

Scales from a hippo playing harp,
playing land grab among the planets
in our universe while we're busy
making other plans.

Hippo angels with mayfly wings
unable to rise above the floodlights
often wonder: Was it worth it?

Then visitors from a distant galaxy
arrive with dibs on an island,
one of the remaining tropical few,
despite typhoon teeth tearing dignity
from the faux scales of a hippo
playing harp & grab ass with all
the planets in our solar system.

5

Inside the neon lights of the dancehall,
eyes and teeth go on tearing
with their little purple knives.

–Ye Chun

BLACK WOOLY

Black wooly ripples our backyard concrete porch pad just below overgrown Autumn grasses tasseled by magenta oil beads igniting each sprouted stalk. This wooly ripples her fur against the sun's early morning switchblades & traverses our patio undulation by undulation, galloping under, over & in between magenta sprigs. Only this wooly isn't black as she ignites copper ribs with each undulation. Zebra rust singeing her fur this wooly traverses a faded garden hose tangled like a fifty-foot garter snake—garden hose thin as a small intestine & knotted into a forgotten Pollock masterpiece. As she wobbles the patio's ledge, I prepare to document her diminutive miracle. But when I look down, she's gone!

ALAN BRITT

THE PRESENT IS THE FUTURE & THE FUTURE IS NOW

I wish I could remember all the fleeting moments of beauty & serenity
experienced in my life,
>   but,
>   alas,
>   I cannot.

So, I write poems.

You write to preserve memories?

Heavens, no. I write to create them.

EMERGENCY ROOM

BUTTERSCOTCH FIRE DEPARTMENT BLUES

(After Otis Taylor)

Major notes twisted
into scorpions,
minor Gilas.

Santa Cruz tilts & spits—
as a coon hound gouges
her nails into the wooden
bed of a scratched
& dented Army
green Dodge pick-up
to its waist in what
some call the tar pits
of modern society.

Still, some say we're dreaming,
as Otis hammers three more
nails into the Crown.

ALAN BRITT

ANNIVERSARY

(RIP: 12/8/1980)

You can tighten green drawstrings,
cuttlefish cauliflower, plus
various shades of indigo mango,
but sooner than later you'll
need magenta solar flares
to combat those pesky mosquitos
symbolizing what you expected
but feared—disappointing life
cemented beneath safety deposits
yellowed by neglect, by familial
& non-familial crises, poverties
impossible to imagine.

Still, time sends its vermilion howl
through midnight saguaros, or coyote
plutonium signaling an eclipse
that resembles empathetic fate, after
all, & not that dreadful creature
attempting to digest Riding Hood,
Hansel, Cinderella, Alice, or the
sleight-of-hand rocker who warned us
ages ago that life is what happens to us
while we're busy making other plans—
yes, you & I knew, that's why we cradled
guitars & gel pens ergonomically
between index, middle & rings honoring
dignity for the universe, pretty much.

EMERGENCY ROOM

FRIDAY NIGHT BLUES

(After John Primer)

Like machetes slicing sugarcane,
guitars sniff the silky surface
before tasting the residue
of sweet smoky roots.

Nervous hands of ice,
like the day they dragged
the two of us into this god
forsaken universe.

Like ancestors' pies, piping rhubarb,
gooseberry, & that quintessential
ugly peach pie, plus cornbread &
Navy beans to survive the war years.

Like there's this crow
surrounded by townsfolk
& everyone's slamming mezcal,
& crow tries his best to keep up,
but it's useless.

It's just like that, just about
the time primordial scales
sheared off me one by one.

ALAN BRITT

It's just like that but not like
that anymore—rubber thorns,
mostly, plus a few ovulating
hibiscus stamens—not enough
to make me wheeze, no lasting harm,
really, no more than that, hardly
more than that.

EMERGENCY ROOM

TWO POETS

What happened to the two poets I call Mutt & Jeff? You call them what you like, but I call them Mutt & Jeff. Mutt grew so popular that he eventually lost a step or two. He purchased condos in New Jersey & ate at white napkin restaurants, while Jeff was shunned for being blunt. In a culture that reveres fairy dust, one who speaks his mind, as Billy warned us generations ago, "will be avoided." So, Jeff, isolated with obsessions that little by little burrowed into his poems the way larvae cauterize crabapples, or the way palmetto bugs strip forest greens & banana yellows from acid free watercolors smeared & dabbed into space & time by refined horsehair—In any event, isolation infused Jeff's poems with habanero & poison oak.

The above is a fairytale but a tale of two poets in the Great Experiment struggling to survive the trolling nets of the Empire. Two poets, living many lives before, in other cultures, other dreams, their ochre fingers charred on El Castillo Cave walls, etching & scratching DNA into whatever allowed them to survive.

Both men remember, forget, remember to forget, then some days nothing.

NOT TODAY

In the spirit of Juan Ramón, Alan announces that he's not at home to receive nasty crows—actually, he understands why crows get nasty, so crows are welcome—but vermin charities that expense limousines to conferences in glass buildings during trips to South of France & tropical isles (in particular) to "wipe out poverty" while fleecing the fucking poor. No visitors today. No mechanical ticking heartbeat draining the humanitarian psyche, each raspy click of industrial eyeball urging, *Get up & greet the day with a smile*, each click an empty chamber on a Russian revolver. Today's a dried magnolia leaf→neighbor's mower clunks maple debris while tangoing every twist & turn beyond my bedroom window before fading & returning with a 45-caliber growl. Alas, no carpet bagging, no political tea bagging, no Baudelaire's "You must get high!" nonsense, no venturing into streets littered with Halloween wrappers herding cultures into diabetes & cancer for the machine to siphon one last Wheat Penny for rich wizards behind the curtain to, oh, Jesus Christ, it never ends! Yes, we need Jesus, over & over. But, do you think we'd nail him again for altering our DNA? Hell, we stole his name—after nailing him & bloodstaining a humanity unable to refute his wisdom. Like spoiled children, we tore his arms & legs off the way adolescents dismantle a garden spider before tossing it down a well. So, like hypocrites declare, "Because I can't support your gay lifestyle, etcetera, I cannot in good conscience (whatever that is) tip you for serving me fries, liquid diabetes, & cheesecake, today, so here is your tip: *Go to Church!*, at the very moment Bill Maher urges folks to *retrieve their proselytizing $20 bills from that fecal covered velvet collection plate next Sunday & make those douchebags go out & earn a living like the rest of us!* Feeling better already.

EMERGENCY ROOM

TRANSFORMATION

(For Duda Penteado)

We the people, indigenous atoms
splintered & chipped by cannon balls
but reborn as bursts of wild Gloxinia
or Formosa bougainvillea.

Point is, we decorate a tapestry
of quantum genocide—inch by
inch, law by law.

Point is, the Brazilian jaguar, eyes
of granite arrow tips symbolizing
visions of egalitarian pulp
& palmetto angels strolling rain
forests not yet suffocated
by political cigar smoke.

But we breathe the same air,
piss in reservoirs owned by
OGX & CCX, aka EBX.

Point is, we love our ancestors,
our feral uncles, cousins, angelic
mothers, & dreaming sisters.

Point is, despite our conch shells
powdered into doubt
& deconstructed from birth,
we remain vibrant, celebratory

ALAN BRITT

Brugmansia trumpets
of wisdom scouring the roots
of terra Brasilia, Father Earth!

WINTER

(For Andrew Accario & the Bruised Apple Bookstore)

White mink scampers snow drifts
like Desdemona dragging her silk scarf
across a crystal skull.

Six inches of blue snow carpenter tool-
trimmed from the razored edges
of a whitewashed horizon.

Vestiges of words, non-gluten words,
organic, Jurassic Age words that glitter;
& just when we thought, from nowhere,
it seems, words glitter.

VIOLIN SMOKE

(For Paul Sohar)

From his cave in Granada, King gypsy tells an aging lover that when you fall in love but are not loved in return, an ironic encounter with ecstasy arrives in the seductive form of Duende. When the old lover hears this, the fountain with marble angels turns green. The old man has loved for several thousand years. His love, fluid yet geometric, contains winged black mussel shells & a blonde liqueur flowing from the breasts of an algae-coated nymph dipping her fingers into a pond of coy. His love is a loon howling below the moon's tin shoulders. Duende like a wasp enters the old man's skin. Not upon or below but inside his skin the wasp dreams the old man's dreams. The wasp buzzes the old man's skull & burns like a candle in his throat before this Duende slithers like a fish across the old man's eyeballs. A red octopus betrays the old man's lips when he speaks of love while King gypsy adjusts his fan-backed rattan chair woven around alkaloid iron. The old man's fingers turn to Spanish moss when he squeezes the wind's ivory waist. His unrequited love tastes of absinthe, & with eyes like white scorpions it plunders his paper mâché soul vibrating the ether.

EMERGENCY ROOM

PTERODACTYL FUTURE

Pterodactyl claw of pollen singes
my eyelash, sends a quiver to my
mammalian brain that rain
or some other meteorological
phenomenon is a matter of faith
& not my model for the future.

Cotton fibers separate the fingertips
of my thoughts—I wonder who
freezes because of shifting breezes
stirred by the thundering herd?

Fairy from an Irish tale lingers, wings
dissolving like rainbows on a bubble
& hidden behind whole grain sans gluten
conversations rustling a distant room
with a conch shell ambiance fit for prince
or princess in some Jurassic brine
surging oblongata lava.

Pterodactyl claw of pollen singes
my eyelash, sends a quiver to my
mammalian brain that rain
or some other meteorological
phenomenon remains a matter of faith
& not my model for the future.

87

ALAN BRITT

THE CRUELEST MONTH

Blue jay creaks a corroded porch swing.

Future's fingertips like transients
cocooned along the London Tube.

Angelic orders of freshly laundered aspirations
slapped by the rusty hinges of a Southern wind that
tattoos rainbows across Atlantic dolphinfish,
(aka mahi-mahi) whose Cubist heads exceeding
evolution vaporize into a Matisse afterbirth.

Twisted Black Forest cane taps leaden segmented
windows, its demented brass tip upsetting au pairs
pouring steaming tomato, garlic & basil
from copper saucepans over pasta al dente.

Banana fronds for eyelids & Red Cross helicopters
like dragonflies hovering the paddies
flattened into jade salvation,
into grey hairs sallowing cheekbones,
until a hand is a torch,
an oily rag lit by grief,
a hand a torch, typhoons like fists,
a hand a torch,
napalm compressed like a diamond
& leaking from the black & white eyes
of Walter Cronkite, David Brinkley,
& that sister from Des Moines who lost
             her baby brother

88

EMERGENCY ROOM

to a booby trap of congressional lies,
a hand a torch,
not a pig in a Geico commercial
but a real live stinging nettles
& gypsy lifeline creases in the palm torch.

EMERGENCY ROOM

Notes

Part 1: Epigraph by Federico García Lorca translated by Christopher Sawyer Lauçanno from papers by Christopher Sawyer Lauçanno relating to Federico García Lorca

Page 3: Epigraph from *Of Flies and Monkeys/de Singes et de mooches* by Jacques Dupin (Translated from the French by John Taylor), The Bitter Oleander Press, Fayetteville, NY: 2014

Page 12: Epigraph from "We Almost Lost Detroit" by Gil Scott-Heron. *No Nukes*. Elektra Records: 1997

Part 2: Epigraph by Marsh River—one afternoon stretched out beneath a blade of sunlight, Marsh River spoke his epiphany to me after I lamented that humans, because of their selfish nature, were destroying themselves and planet Earth simultaneously.

Page 22: Epigraph from Pablo Neruda from his *Canto General*, specifically from Canto II: *Las Alturas de Macchu Picchu (The Heights of Macchu Picchu)* published in Mexico by Talleres Gráficos de la Nación: 1950

Page 36: Lyrics from "Just Gimme Some Truth" by John Lennon. *Imagine.* Apple Records: 1971

Part 3: Epigraph by Sean Frederick Forbes, "Series Editor's Note" from *Black Lives Have Always Mattered: A Collection of Essays, Poems and Personal Narratives*, Oyewole, Abiodun, Editor, 2LeafPress, New York: 2017

Page 47: Epigraph by Wm. Shakespeare Jones from his introduction to *Universal Verse*, edited by Sylvia Salinas, Wildlife Communications, San Pedro, Jupiter: 2001

Part 4: Epigraph by W. B. Yeats from his poem "The Second Coming" that appeared in *The Dial*, November 1920

Page 59: Punctum (point of impact of the image) being unique to the response of the individual viewer of the image. *Punctum* punctuates *the*

91

ALAN BRITT

studium (deconstruction of the image) and as a result pierces its viewer. To allow the *punctum* effect, the viewer must repudiate all conventionally imposed knowledge. –Roland Barthes

Page 65: Epigraph from "Punish the Monkey" by Mark Knopfler. *Kill to Get Crimson*. Mercury Records/Warner Brothers: 2008.

Page 70: Epigraph from "Ode on a Grecian Urn" written by John Keats in May 1819 and published anonymously January 1820 in *Annals of the Fine Arts* (issue 15)

Part 5: Epigraph by Ye Chun from her poem "Goodfellas Bar" from her book, *Travel Over Water*, The Bitter Oleander Press, Fayetteville, NY: 2005

Alan Britt has published 20 books of poetry with poems appearing in *Agni Review, American Poetry Review, The Bitter Oleander, Bloomsbury Review, Christian Science Monitor, Confrontation, Cottonwood, English Journal, Epoch, Flint Hills Review, International Gallerie* (India), *Irodalmi Jelen* (Hungary), *Kansas Quarterly, Letras* (Chile), *Magyar Naplo* (Hungary), *Midwest Quarterly, Minnesota Review, Missouri Review, New Letters, A New Ulster* (Ireland), *Northwest Review, Osiris, Pedrada Zurda* (Ecuador), *Poet's Market, Queen's Quarterly* (Canada), *Revista/Review Interamericana* (Puerto Rico), *Revista Solar* (Mexico), *Roanoke Review, Stand* (UK), *Steaua* (Romania), *Sunstone, Tulane Review, Verse Daily, Wasafiri* (UK), and *Zaira Journal* (Philippines). He was nominated for the 2021 International Janus Pannonius Prize awarded by the Hungarian Centre of PEN International for excellence in poetry from any part of the world. Previous nominated recipients include Lawrence Ferlinghetti, Charles Bernstein and Yves Bonnefoy. He interviewed at The Library of Congress for *The Poet and the Poem* and served as Art Agent for Andy Warhol Superstar, the late great Ultra Violet, while often reading poetry at her Chelsea, New York studio. A graduate of the Writing Seminars at Johns Hopkins University he currently teaches English/Creative Writing at Towson University.

Publications by Alan Britt

Books
Emergency Room
Optical Illusions
Dream Highway
Gunpowder for Single-ball Poems
Ode to Nothing/Óda a semmihez (bilingual)
     Translated into Hungarian by Paul Sohar
Violin Smoke/*Heged füst* (bilingual)
     Translated into Hungarian by Paul Sohar
Lost Among the Hours
Parabola Dreams: *Poems by Silvia Scheibli and Alan Britt*
Alone with the Terrible Universe
Greatest Hits
Hurricane
Vegetable Love
Vermilion
Infinite Days
Amnesia Tango
Bodies of Lightning
The Afternoon of the Light
I Suppose the Darkness Is Ours
Ashes in the Flesh
I Ask for Silence, Also

Anthologies (Editor)
We Are You: Poetry
Alianza: 5 U.S. Poets in Ecuador
Mantras: An Anthology of Immanentist Poetry

ALAN BRITT

Poetry Journal (Editor/Publisher)
Black Moon: Poetry of Imagination

Editor-in-Chief/Poetry Editor/Associate Editor
We Are You Project International
The Loch Raven Review
Ethos Literary Journal (India)

Miscellaneous
Poetry and the Concept of Maya by David Churchill
  (Based upon the poetry of Alan Britt)

CPSIA information can be obtained
at www.ICGtesting.com
Printed in the USA
BVHW082049200622
640215BV00001B/75